# Bavarian drinking games

CW01073036

"An intelligent man is sometimes forced to be drunk to

spend time with his fools"

*Ernest Hemingway*


„I bin solang no net bsuffa, solang i no am Boden ling ko,

one mi festhoitn z´miassen"

*Man in Lederhos´n*

# Bavarian
## drinking games

Autor: Dirk Mayer

**Bibliographic information of the German Library:**

The German Library lists this publication in the German National Bibliography. Detailed bibliographical data are available on the internet at http://dnb.ddb.de.

**Dirk Mayer:**
Bavarian drinking games

Find us on Facebook! (Bavarian Drinking Games)

ISBN 9783839199886

Prouction and publisher: Books on Demand GmbH, Norderstedt

# Table of Contents

# The Reason

What motivated me to write this book?

While backpacking around the globe I often found myself meeting different kinds of people. Nights with them would be especially fun when one of these strangers would introduce a drinking game from home. Suddenly, everyone opened up and it became much easier to communicate and interact, even with the backpacking scene already being very social. In some cases, these nights resulted in great and long-lasting international friendships. Since then, I have come to believe that playing drinking games is actually one of the best ways to meet people.

My experiences in various situations remain unforgotten and I would like to use this book to pass these on. I hope - in fact, I know - that the Reader will enjoy those unforgettable evenings too.

Bavaria is a very special region in which traditions are still adhered to and passed down through generations. The language, traditional costumes and way of life is distinct and a point of pride for our people. Drinking good beer is part of that way of life and I hope with this book to impart some of that tradition to you.

Enjoy the games I experienced living in Bavaria mixed with games that I collected travelling around the world!

## Eins, zwei, drei, gsuffa!

("One, two, three, let's get drunk" – popular Bavarian toast at the Oktoberfest)

The Warning

I want to stress yet again that this book neither demands alcohol consumption nor does it condone or trivialise alcohol abuse.

Information about side effects of alcohol can be found at: http://en.wikipedia.org/wiki/Substance_abuse

**Games introduced in this book are for individuals of drinking age only!**

Please make sure not to submit to or exert peer pressure and to be mindful of your own alcohol consumption.

The majority of games can also be played with non-alcoholic beverages – without lessening the fun.

# Disclaimer

The author does not take any responsibility for the validity, completeness and up-to-dateness of the information provided in this book.

Liability claims, concerning damages of material or immaterial manner that are created by using or not using the information presented in this work are not the responsibility of the author.

Please play the games included in this book at your own risk.

## Facebook Group

I would be delighted to receive feedback, especially about individual games: how you liked them, how you play them, different variations and of course, your own drinking game suggestions!

For this purpose, I have set up the Facebook group "Bavarian Drinking Games". There you can leave comments, suggestions and ideas for games.

# The Rating System

Each game has been rated. The ratings – glasses for drinking games, stars for party games – give you a feel for what to expect.

Here is the ratings breakdown:

**Drinking games**

| | |
|---|---|
| ▼ ▼ ▼ | High speed, high level of drinking |
| ▼ ▼ | Medium speed, medium level of drinking |
| ▼ | Players are "punished" moderately, punishments are distributed equally |

**Party games**

| | |
|---|---|
| ★ ★ ★ | Game offers great entertainment and is perfectly suited for large groups |
| ★ ★ | Game can be crazy or civil depending on how you decide to play it |
| ★ | Nice, sociable game |

# The Games

# King Ludwig II

**Number of players:**   3 – 8

**Resources:**   Deck of cards

**Booze-factor:**   Y Y Y

## Preparation:

For this game you need a deck of cards. The cards are shuffled and stacked.

The player, who has spent the most time without vomiting, starts.

## Rules:

The player whose turn it is draws a card from the deck and places it in the middle of the table. Each card has its own special meaning:

**Card    Meaning**

**2       Two - For you**

The player can choose any player to empty a shot.


**3       Three - For me**

The player has to empty a shot himself.

## 4 Four - Touch the floor

All the players try to touch the floor with their left hand as quickly as possible. The player who is last has to empty a shot.

## 5 Never ever

The player says something that they have never done in their whole life. For example: "I never had sex in an elevator." All participants who have actually experienced that, are punished with a shot.

## 6 Make a rule

The player is allowed to establish a rule, for example: Players aren´t allowed to address each other by their own names anymore, but they must use street names. Or, the words drink, drank and drunk can´t be vocalized anymore. If someone breaks that rule they have to drink immediately. The rule is replaced by another rule when 6 is thrown again

## 7 Sevens

The players have to count clockwise beginning with 1. Every time, a number which is divisible by 7 or has a 7 in it comes up, the player cannot say it out loud. Instead the number has to be replaced by another word or expression, chosen by the player who drew the card. The player must use this word and cannot say any number.

Additionally, the direction of counting changes every time the word or expression is used. For example if the expression is *Wolpertinger* and the counting is clockwise, when someone says the word the counting changes to counter-clockwise. If someone breaches this rules they are punished at once. Of course, a more difficult number could be chosen instead of 7.

## 8     Eight – Pick a mate

The player has to drink but is allowed to choose someone else at the table who has to drink from their glass for as long as the first player does. If the challenged player puts down their glass too early they have to drink one more shot as punishment.

## 9     Nine - Make a rhyme

The player whose turn it is thinks about a short sentence, for example: "I am the winner". Clockwise, every player has to form a rhyme with this sentence, for example: "Let´s go for dinner". If no rhyme comes to mind within five seconds for a player or if someone repeats a sentence, they have to suffer the consequences with a full shot glass.

## 10     Categories

The player mentions a category, for example "blond girls". One after the other, every player has to name an item that fits into this category, such as "Pamela Anderson", "Marilyn Monroe or "Gwen Stefani". If a player doesn´t come up with an idea in five seconds or they repeat something, they are punished appropriately.

## Jack     Only the guys

All male participants drink.

## Queen     Only the chicks

All female participants drink.

## King     Kings

The whole table shouts "Prost!" or "Zum Wohl!", bumps glasses and drinks together.

## Ace     Ace - Touch your face

All players touch their right hand to their left cheek as quickly as possible. The last one drinks.

### Joker   Mr Choice

The joker can be changed into any of the cards and carries with it the consequences of that card.

After every punishment a new card is revealed by the next player.

## Alternatives:

### Card   Meaning

### Joker   Toilet master

The player is appointed as the toilet master. From now on all the players have to ask them for permission to go to the toilet. Depending on their mood they can give their fellow players mercy or take revenge and prohibit them from visiting the bathroom until the next joker is revealed. Then the player has to hope that the next player doesn´t take revenge on them!

### Joker   Mr Obvious

The player inserts a gesture, for example picking their nose. Every time, this gesture is repeated throughout the game the other players have to imitate it as fast as possible. The player who reacts the slowest has to drink.

### 6     Make a rule

In the normal version of this game, every 6 dealt creates a new rule that replaces the previous one. However, with this alternative, every 6 dealt create a new rule in addition to the previous one. Rules add up and creat chaos.

## Result:

The combination of strict rules and the opportunity for creativity give this game its special balance and make it a favourite of the author.

# Vomit into bucket

**Number of players:**   3 – 8

**Resources:**   Bucket or pot

**Booze-factor:**   Y Y Y

## Preparation:

The most important piece of equipment for this game is a bucket or large
pot (the more players the bigger it should be). It is placed in the middle of
the table.

## Rules:

This game has different rounds. In the first round the player with the
shortest forefinger (pointer) starts. In all the following rounds the loser
begins.

The first player puts their **left** forefinger onto the edge of pot. Then the
other participants follow clockwise. If someone puts their finger onto the
edge of the pot before the player in front of them, they are immediately
punished with a shot. Nervous and overly-hasty fingers result in some
players jumping the queue and this makes for some quick drinking.

Every breach of the rules is immediately punished by a shot and after
every breach of the rules a new round begins. The loser starts the round
Strict adherence to the rules is important for a smooth game.

The placement of the right forefinger on the edge of the pot also counts as a breach of the rules.

Once all forefingers are placed on the edge of the pot, the real game begins. The player who started the round has to call out a number. As they are calling out the number (that is at the same exact moment) each player can choose between two possible actions.

**Action 1: A player could leave their finger on the edge of the pot.**

**Action 2: A player could raise their finger.**

If the number called out is the same as the number of fingers remaining on the edge of the pot, the first player can relax and doesn't have to drink (If it is wrong they must continue in the round). Everyone except this player places their fingers back onto the edge of the pot. The game continues, and the player to the left calls out another number. If the guess is correct, they can relax out of the round with the first player. If the guess is wrong, however, they stay within the round and it's their left neighbor's turn.

If there is no breach of the rules the game keeps going until there are only two players left. If either of them makes a correct guess the round is over. The player on the left is the round's loser and has to drink.

If a player is too slow in their reactions or tries to cheat or argue with the others they are immediately punished with a shot. At the moment that a player is calling out a number the others should not react to the number but should be spontaneous.

## Overview of breaches of the rules:

| | |
|---|---|
| **Breach 1:** | Jumping the queue in the clockwise placing of forefingers onto the edge of the pot |
| **Breach 2:** | Placing the right forefinger on the edge of the pot |
| **Breach 3:** | Raising the finger too slowly as a number is called out |
| **Breach 4: (Alternative 1)** | Punishments take longer than 5 seconds. |

**Breach 5:**
**(Alternative 2)** Placing of fingers takes longer than 5 seconds

## Alternatives:

### (1) "5-seconds-punishment"

If someone takes a long time taking a shot, they have to take two. Players quit arguing and drink fast rather than risk two shots.

### (2) "5-seconds-time-limit"

Every player who is in turn to put their finger on the edge of the pot cannot take longer than five seconds to do so.

It is advisable to count only the fourth and fifth second out-loud, then the decision is not that arbitrary, but there is plenty of room for error.

## Result:

"Vomit into a bucket" is chaotic but successful when the rules are followed. Fun is guaranteed when every breach of the rules is punished immediately.

If there are some players who can't stop cheating a referee could be chosen to make sure the rules are followed. If the role of referee rotates, the game is fairer, but can be more dramatic due to revenge tactics.

It is interesting to observe how as the night wears on and several rounds pass, the numbers called out become mathematically ridiculous and their accuracy is inversely correlated with drunkenness.

# Ladyfinger

**Number of players:**   3 – 8

**Equipment:**   2 - 3 packs of ladyfingers and 2 die

**Booze-factor:**   🍸 🍸 🍸

## Preparation:

This game is played with 2 die. The player who is able to eat the most ladyfingers in one minute starts the game. Ensure that there is one ladyfinger left for each player.

## Rules:

The players throw the two die in turns, clockwise. The rolled numbers have the following meaning:

### Number seven

All the players have to direct their ladyfinger to their tip of their nose with their left hand as quickly as possible while screaming "Ladyfingers" out loud. The player, who takes the longest time or uses their right hand, has to drink a shot.

### Number nine

The neighbour to the left of the player who rolled the die has to empty a shot.

## Number eleven

The neighbour to the right of the player who rolled the die has to empty a shot.

## All ones, all twos, all threes, all fours, all fives

The rolled number (not the sum) decides how many shots the player can allocate to the other players.

For example in case of "all fives" the player who rolled can give 2 shots to one player and 3 shots to another one. If they hold a grudge against a certain player, they have the possibility to give all 5 shots to that player.

## All sixes

In case of rolling "all sixes", in addition to allocating 6 shots to the others, the player is allowed to establish a rule.

Ideally the new rule is associated with a rolled number, for example from now on every player who rolls a 2 has to do a little Bavarian dance (for example a *Schuhblattler*) for the others or yodel at the top of their lungs for a couple of minutes. Here the creativity of each player is required.

## One or both die show a three

The player is appointed "Ladyfinger". Whenever a 3 is rolled from now on the "Ladyfinger" has to drink. If two 3´s are rolled the "Ladyfinger" must drink twice. The "Ladyfinger" must continue this way until they roll one or two 3´s again. They can then choose someone new to carry the title.

## Other numbers

The remaining numbers don't have a special meaning, the game continues and no one drinks.

## Alternatives:

### (1) "Soft all sixes"

In the case of throwing "all sixes" there are still 6 shots to be allocated, but now the new rule replaces the old one. Thus there are less rules to be followed and the error- and punishment-rate declines.

### (2) Over the edge

If one dice falls off the table during a roll, the clumsy player has to empty a shot immediately.

Note: Sometimes players don't want to follow the rules and search for excuses. To make "Ladyfinger" really fun, everyone should adhere to the rules and treat each other fairly as they get more and more drunk.

## Result:

You will soon discover your hidden talents and that some of you are Schuhblatter kings and yodel queens.

# Rascal

**Number of players:** 3 – 6

**Resources:** None

**Booze-factor:** 🍸 🍸

## Preparation:

At the beginning of the game each player selects a fruit. To familiarize the group with each player and their fruit, each player repeats their fruit clockwise two or three times.

## Rules:

The player who attracted the most negative attention the last evening out starts.

It is their task to call out the fruity name of one of the other players three times. It´s their choice whether they want to just come out and say the name of the fruit three times or if they want to cleverly integrate it into a story they tell, like for example an anecdote about their grandmother´s picnic basket at her 75th birthday.

To pronounce one player´s fruity name is an attack against that player. In total each player has two chances to attack any fruit in the round. It doesn´t have to be the same fruit both times. After one failed attempt the can try another fruit for their second attack.

The attacked player can defend themself by calling out their own fruity name once before the offender has finished their third repetition of the fruit. If the defender can't manage to protect themselves, they must empty a shot and they become the next attacker. An attacker may attack two people at the same time in order to try to confuse them and increase their chances of success.

If, in contrast, both attacks are defended successfully and the attacker hasn't fulfilled their mission, they have to drink. After that they have another two attacks. If they fail again they have to drink two shots and their left neighbor starts.

## Alternatives:

The game gets especially fruity if the players aren't called by their real names but by their fruity names for the duration of the game.

For example, a player would say " Banana, could you pass me that bottle opener?" If someone breaks the rule and uses real names, they have to drink.

It's unbelievable how many players find it difficult to follow this rule, especially as they become drunker and drunker.

## Result:

The game is at its best potential late at night. Good hearing is important, and choosing a monosyllabic fruit increases your chances of preventing attacks.

# Quarters

**Number of players:** 3 – 6

**Equipment:** Coins and an ashtray

**Booze-/Party-factor:** Y Y Y

## Preparation:

Each player needs a 20 or 25 cent coin (amateurs can use a 5 cent coin as well). The ashtray is placed in the middle of the table. Alternatively, a container with a low rim can be used.

## Rules:

The player with the least amount of cash in their pocket begins. Their task is to get the coin into the ashtray. For the player to succeed, the coin must touch the table exactly once before reaching the ashtray. That is, the coin must bounce once before landing in the ashtray.

If the player manages to do this, they may select one of the other players to drink a shot of hard liquor.

If the player fails, they are given a second try. However, they don't have to take that chance and are free to pass the coin on to their neighbour to the left. If they try for a second time and succeed, they can choose another player to drink a shot. If they fail on the second attempt, however, they must drink.

As long as the coin lands in the ashtray at each attempt, the player may go on throwing the coin. Whoever manages to land a coin in the ashtray three times (during one turn) is allowed to introduce a new rule to the game. This could be, for instance, that each player has to stand up when throwing the coin and afterwards needs to sit down again. Subsequently, every player who does not adhere to this new rule is punished with a shot (or in an alternative version, with taking off a piece of clothing).

Once a player has introduced a new rule, the game continues with the next player to the left. The new rule is valid for the duration of the game.

## Alternatives:

### (1) Double Quarters

Semi-professionals may want to attempt to bounce the coin multiple times before landing it in the ashtray. The number of times the coin hits the table then equals the amount of shots the other players have to drink as punishment.

### (2) Mud Quarters

If one of the players spills the precious liquor when pouring the punishment shots, they are punished themselves. The table cannot be cleaned. There is no such thing as easily flipping a coin on a sticky surface…

## Result:

Practice hard and *lass sie bluten*!

# Black Finger

**Number of players:**    3 – 6

**Equipment:**    Matchboxes

**Booze-factor:**    ▼ ▼

## Preparation:

For this game several matchboxes are needed.

## Rules:

The player who hasn´t been laid the longest begins. They light a match and pass it directly to their neighbour on the left. That player also passes the match to their neighbour, but the second player has the choice of deciding when to pass on the lit match. The same goes for all the following players.

At any time, when the match has almost burnt down, the situation gets very tricky for someone. If one player doesn´t manage to pass on the match before it goes out or before they drop it in order to not burn their fingers, they are punished by a shot immediately.

Note: Highly advised, if the match is still lit on the floor put it out!

If a player is next to take the match, they must take it no matter how far it´s burnt down. Whoever breaks this rule has to drink as well.

The player who had to drink is the one to start the new round and lights a new match.

## Overview of breach of the rules:

**Breach 1**     Match falls to the floor or table.

**Breach 2**     Match extinguishes.

**Breach 3**     The player refuses to take the match from another player.

## Alternatives:

You can boost the thrill by lighting two matches at the same time.
The first match is lit by the loser of the previous round, the other one is lit by the guy who is sitting across from them. There is no given order, therefore it is possible that one player gets two matches from their two neighbours at the same time. In this situation they can either pass the matches to their neighbours on either side or they can give both matches to one player.

If the player drops or lets both matches go out they have to empty two shots, of course!

## Result:

Drunken debauchery and black fingers.

Please be extremely cautious in this game as fire and alcohol are present! Be sensible and play the game on a fire proof surface (no shag carpeting!).

In addition it is advised to not use hard liquor as a punishment drink because it´s flammable! The game is entertaining enough with any other spiked drink.

# Stinky Fish

**Number of players:**     3 – 6

**Resources:**     5 die

**Booze-factor:**     

## Preparation:

To decide who is the first to play, all players throw the dice one after another, using all 5 die. Whoever rolls the first "fish" gets to start the game. Rolling a "fish" means having no dice showing either a 1 or 5, as well no number more than twice (no triples). For example, an acceptable roll would be: 2,4,4,3,6. If more than one player has a "fish", the fishiest one, that is the smelliest, may begin.

## Rules:

All players roll the dice clockwise, using all five die. Depending on the numbers they throw, they can obtain the following points:

| | |
|---|---|
| **1** | 100 points |
| **5** | 50 points |
| Fish = no 1 and 5 and no triple numbers | 0 points |

If a player rolls triples, they are awarded the following points:

| | |
|---|---|
| **Triple 1´s** | 100 x 2 x 2 = 400 points |

| Triple 3´s | 300 points |
|---|---|
| Triple 4´s | 400 points |
| Triple 5´s | 50 x 2 x 2 = 200 points |
| Triple 6´s | 600 points |
| | |
| Quadruple 1´s | 100 x 2 x 2 x 2 = 800 points |
| Quadruple 2´s | 200 x 2 = 400 points |
| Quadruple 3´s | 300 x 2 = 600 points |
| Quadruple 4´s | 400 x 2 = 800 points |
| Quadruple 5´s | 50 x 2 x 2 x 2 = 400 points |
| Quadruple 6´s | 600 x 2 = 1200 points |
| | |
| Quintuple 1´s | 100 x 2 x 2 x 2 x 2 = 1600 points |
| Quintuple 2´s | 200 x 2 x 2 = 800 points |
| Quintuple 3´s | 300 x 2 x 2 = 1200 points |
| Quintuple 4´s | 400 x 2 x 2 = 1600 points |
| Quintuple 5´s | 50 x 2 x 2 x 2 x 2 = 800 points |
| Quintuple 6´s | 600 x 2 x 2 = 2400 points |

Important: A player has to roll at least 50 more points than the player before them. If they fail, they must drink one shot of hard liquor. The next player then starts at 0 points.

As long as a player obtains points from their rolls, they can continue rolling and racking up the points. After each roll, those die that have been rewarded with points are put aside and the player continues with the remaining die. Once all die have been rewarded points and thus "used", the points are added up. If, at any time, a roll fails to produce points, the player´s turn is over and the points are added up.

If a player throws a "fish", they must drink one shot of hard liquor and they lose all their points. The following player starts with 0 points and therefore doesn't have to exceed anybody's score. They can throw anything (except a fish) to move on.

If a players succeeds in obtaining points with all five die, regardless of whether they do so in their first roll or in subsequent rolls, they may start over with all five dice. All points obtained will then be added to their previous points.

Each player can decide if they want to continue throwing the remaining die once they have exceeded the previous player´s points. By continuing the game they can raise the bar for the following players (of course, with every additional dice that is put aside the risk for obtaining zero points increases).

If a player rolls double 5´s (50x2 = 100 points) they may switch one of the die to a 1 (100 points) and put it aside. The other dice can then be used for the next roll.

**Here's an example to illustrate the rules:**

**Player A** starts the round by rolling the following numbers: 1,4,3,2,5
This equals 150 points (1 = 100 + 5 = 50 points).
He puts the 1 and 5 aside.
Since he is the first player in this round he doesn't have to out-roll anyone, he decides not to continue and therefore hands over the dice to the next player, **player B**.

**Player B** throws the following numbers in her first roll: 2,5,4,4,5
This equals 100 points (5 = 50 + 5 = 50).
**Player B** has to obtain at least 50 points more than the previous player, player A, i.e. 200 points. So far she has achieved only 100 points, thus she still needs another 100 points. She switches one of the 5´s to a 1, then she puts this one aside and continues with the remaining four die.
She rolls: 4,1,4,4.
This equals 500 points (three times 4 = 400 + 1 = 100). Up until now, she had obtained 100 points. Together with the 500 points from her last throw she now has 600 points. Since she obtained these points with all five of her die she may now start over again, or she can decide to pass on the die. She decides to roll again for glory. Now she rolls the following numbers: 2,3,6,6,4. She risked too much and rolled a "fish"! All points she had obtained previously are lost and she is punished with a shot of hard liquor.

## Alternatives:

**"Fishy business"**

A real fish is brought along and put in the middle of the table. Each time player rolls a "fish" they have to drink a shot. On top of that they must put the fish underneath their shirt until another "fish" is rolled. At the end of the game the fish is fried and eaten with parsley potatoes. Alternatively, a used sock or even some panties can be used instead.

## Result:

*Petri heil!*

# Asshole

$1 + 2 + 1 =$

| **Number of players:** | 3 - 8 |
|---|---|
| **Equipment:** | Deck of cards |
| **Party-factor:** | |

## Preparation:

The game is best played with a deck of Bavarian cards. After shuffling and cutting the deck each player is dealt 3 cards.

## Rules:

The player left of the dealer starts the game. They have to place a bid on the number of tricks they think they are going to make with their three cards. The meaning of each hand as well as how to make a trick will be explained later on.

After the first player has placed their bet by raising their hand and indicating the number of tricks by holding up fingers, all other players do so as well, clockwise.

You should keep in mind that there is a total of three tricks in each game. As each player has three cards, a player can make a maximum of three tricks.

The dealer places their bid last. They count all tricks the other players have announced. However, contrary to the other players, the dealer must make a bid so that the total amount of tricks announced at the table does not equal three. That is to say that the dealer can make any bid as long as their bid combined with those of the other players does not add up to three tricks. This rule accounts for the fact that at least one player will not be able to keep up with their bid, automatically providing at least one loser for the game.

A few examples:

## Example 1

Player A announces one trick, player B indicates none and player C states two tricks. This equals three tricks in total. The dealer now places their bid of one trick.

In this case there will be at least one loser as the players have announced four tricks in total while only three tricks maximum would be possible throughout one round.

Of course, the dealer could have announced two or three tricks as well. Their bid depends entirely on the quality of the cards they received in the beginning. However, they would not have been allowed to announce zero tricks, as the total amount of tricks placed by the rest of the players would have equalled three.

The dealer has – even though they aren´t entirely independent in their choice of tricks – a certain advantage over the other players as they are last in the round for the first trick as the cards are revealed they have the opportunity to see what comes before them.

## Example 2

Player A announces one trick, player B also places their bid on one trick and player C indicates no trick at all. This equals two tricks in total. The dealer decides to announce zero tricks. In this case two tricks have been announced.

Keeping in mind the number of cards available (three), this means that one player will obtain one trick more than they previously indicated. Again, one player will automatically be a loser. In addition, the dealer could have announced two or three tricks (four and five tricks in total, respectively).

They couldn't, however, opt for just one trick as this would have equalled the forbidden number of three tricks in total.

After each player now has placed their bid, the player left to the dealer starts playing one of their cards. Clockwise, all players take their turn. The person playing the highest card will receive the trick. In case several cards of the same level have been played, the player who plays the card first will receive the trick.

The cards are to be ranked as follows:
Ace, King, *Ober* (Queen), *Unter* (Jack), 10, 9, 8, 7
(In absence of a Bavarian deck take out the numbers lower than 7)

Analysis of bids and tricks begins. Each player who could not keep up with their initial bid will have to drink a shot of schnapps or another hard alcohol. So, if you bid over or under the number of tricks you win, you must drink!

## Alternatives:

### (1) "Last high card bids"

If several cards with the same rank have been played, the player playing the card last wins the trick (instead of the first).

### (2) "Blind Bid"

The players may only look at their cards after they have placed their bids. They have to announce their tricks "blindly".

## Result:

This game breeds a lot of mischievousness. This can be enhanced if each "loser" is assigned so called asshole-tasks such as cleaning up the trash or having to keep the liquor supply steady. Feel free to choose the tasks you want and feel free to be an asshole about it!

# Kamasutra

| | |
|---|---|
| **Number of players:** | Optional |
| **Resources:** | 3 boxes, pencil and a piece of paper |
| **Party-factor:** | ★ ★ |

## Preparation:

All participants write their names on a small note. The notes are separated by gender and put into 2 boxes. The third box contains notes with the following:

| | |
|---|---|
| • right hand | • left hand |
| • right foot | • left foot |
| • right ear | • left ear |
| • right eye | • left eye |
| • right thigh | • left thigh |
| • chin | • forehead |
| • neck | • ass |

One of the participants is responsible for moderating.

## Rules:

Couples are determined by drawing pairs out of the female and male boxes.

The first couple to be drawn begins. They should move to a central spot in the room where they can be easily seen by the other couples.

The moderator takes two notes out of the third box containing the body parts. They read the note out loud. Now it is the task of the couple to make contact between those two body parts. It is irrelevant which part is chosen by the man and which by the woman.

If, for example, the notes "left hand" and "ass" are drawn, the man could touch the woman's ass or it could happen the other way round. Notes are continually drawn and the couple may have to use all of their body parts in order to carry out the actions. If, by chance, a note with a body part that has already been called out is drawn, then the participant with that body part free must carry out the action. If, however, both are already using that body part the game is over as they have not been able to successfully complete the task.

The couple can try its luck as long as it is able to connect the required body parts without losing the connection between them. At some point the position of the couple will be so bizarre and tangled that the next task cannot be fulfilled. The couple is then out and the number of connections is listed as points. The moderator selects the next couple.

The other players are allowed to help in terms of hints and suggestions, as often how to make a connection between body parts is not evident to the pair.

After all couples have finished their round it's time to identify the winning couple. The highest score is decisive for the victory. A bottle of wine and a passionate kiss between the winning couple is a nice finishing touch to the game.

## Alternatives:

It is possible to play the game in a more exotic version. Try playing it scantily-clad in a swingers club or if that`s a little too risky for you, heed the author's advice and add the following notes to the box…

- breast
- tongue
- stomach
- mouth

The game gets more difficult if the note drawn is pinched between the two connected body parts. The couple loses if one of the notes falls to the floor.

## Result:

This game works especially well with acquaintances or a mixed crowd.
Guaranteed: the night will turn into a party your guests won´t easily forget!

# Stranded

**Number of players:**    3 – 8

**Equipment:**    None

**Booze-factor:**    🍸 🍸

## Preparation:

A moderator, who is the only person who already knows the rules of the game, tells an imaginary story of a ship, in which all the other players are passengers. The ship gets into trouble at sea and starts to sink.

The moderator finishes the story by telling the others that there is an opportunity to save themselves by swimming to a nearby island. Everyone allowed to take two objects with them from the boat. However, only a few objects will allow them to survive on the island.

## Rules:

One after another, the players are asked about the two objects that they to take ashore. If the proposed objects are appropriate, from the moderator point of view, the player is rescued and the game is over for them. If the moderator doesn´t like the proposed objects, however, the player has to one shot and stays in the game.

Each player always makes an argument for their two objects and then it´s next player´s turn. The game continues as long as the moderator agrees every argument.

Which criteria does the moderator use to decide whether the chosen objects will aid in the player's rescue or not? Their decision depends on the first names and last names of the players. If, for example one player was named Christoph Weinzierl, the moderator would accept the objects condom and water.

## Alternatives:

To prevent the players from falling into a drunken stupor the moderator can participate actively in the game as a help. In every round they can name two objects which begin with the initial letters of their first and last name.

In order to continue the game after only one round, new criteria can be invented. For example the first letter of the players' hair colour in combination with an imaginary dirty word.

## Result:

Note that the more challenging the chosen criteria are, the longer the players have to suffer. That's why the moderator should suffer in some way, for example drinking a solidarity-shot every second round as well. In particularly long games, at some point the moderator should offer mercy to the players by identifying the solution.

# Fumbling in the dark

**Number of players:**   15

**Ressources:**   5 chairs

**Party-factor:**   ⭐⭐⭐

## Preparation:

One of the participants who is already familiar with the rules of the game, takes on the role of the moderator.

The moderator places five chairs in the centre of a busy room, ideally at a house party.

## Rules:

The moderator chooses five girls to stand on the chairs.

Then, the moderator chooses five boys, who have the task of identifying the girls by squeezing and feeling their asses blindfolded. The boys have a few minutes to look at the girls asses before being led into another room. They are then told that the order of the girls will be changed and they must leave the room to be blindfolded. The girls are then replaced by five boys from the party audience.

The boys are blindfolded, then brought back into the room and lined up behind the "girls" so that each one is within an arm´s reach. The moderator gives a starting signal and the boys have to try to guess the identity of the "girls" by feeling them.

The real girls who are now part of the audience can watch with pleasure as the boys feel up the other boys´ asses.

Note: In order to keep the joke going for as long as possible, and to ensure that an incriminating video can easily be filmed, the moderator should ensure that the audience doesn´t jeopardize the premise of the game. Shouts such as "hey that´s my girlfriend!" are appropriate, however.

## Result:

Hilarious videos that you can upload to youtube or at least a good time had by all!

# Ace of Hearts drinks

**Number of players:** 3 – 8

**Equipment:** Deck of cards

**Booze-factor:** Y Y Y

## Preparation:

For this game you need a deck of cards. They are shuffled in every new round. The dealer changes clockwise in every round.

## Rules:

In Bavarian slang aces are called "pigs". Naturally, for this game, the player who looks most like a pig, begins. They deal the cards and their le neighbour cuts the deck. The rules for this game are very simple and it makes for a great time when participants are already partially (or fully) drunk.

The dealer flips over one card for each player (including themself), so tha everyone can see them. This continues in rounds until the ace of hearts i placed in front of a player. This player has lost the round immediately. They have to drink a shot and the game starts again.

## Alternatives:

### (1) "Every ace drinks"

To avoid having one lonely loser in every round, you can agree that ever player who is dealt an ace of any suit, drinks. After revealing all the aces the game begins again.

## (2) "Kings pimp, aces drink"

In addition to the aces, the kings become important in the game. If a king is dealt to a player they can choose any alcoholic drink, pour it into a shot glass and dump the shot glass into a *Maß* (beer stein) which is placed in the middle if the table. As soon as the next ace is revealed in front of a player, that player has to empty the glass.

Of course, sometimes the beer stein remains empty as no kings have appeared before an ace. In this case the player is lucky and does not have to drink. Conversely, sometimes four kings appear before an ace and the player must drink all four shots.

# Result:

Easy rules + malicious joy (*Schadenfreude*) = great amusement!

# Drinking pyramid

**Number of players:**     3 – 4

**Hilfsmittel:**     Deck of cards

**Rauschfaktor:**

## Preparation:

For this game you need a deck of international cards. The cards are first shuffled and the player left of the dealer cuts the deck. Each player is dealt five cards. The cards are lined up in front of each player, face down.

Important: The players must keep the cards in the order they are dealt and lined up throughout the game.

When a player gets their cards, they can look at their deck only once. They should try to remember in which order the cards are placed. Suit and color are not important and can be ignored. The player should also ensure that other players do not see their cards.

With the extra cards a pyramid is formed in the middle of the table (see illustration). The cards of the pyramid are also placed face down.

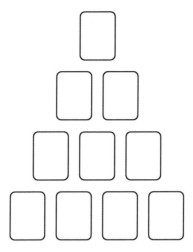

**Illustration: How to build the pyramid**

The remaining cards are neatly stacked next to the pyramid. They will not be used for the rest of this game.

Advice: In this game the players are not punished by full shot glasses, they should only be approximately one mouthful (1 cl).

## Rules:

One player is chosen to be the ruler and Pharaoh of the pyramid. The Pharaoh flips over one of the cards in the bottom line.

Now the "attack phase" begins and the other players can challenge the Pharaoh. An attacking player claims that there is a card in their line of cards that is identical to the chosen card from the pyramid. If the Pharaoh flipped over a jack (knave) for example, a player can claim that there is at least one jack in their cards as well.

Each player can challenge the Pharaoh, despite whether there is really a corresponding card their line of cards or not.

Now, the Pharaoh has two options; they can believe the claim or they can challenge it.

If they choose to believe the claim, they must drink a shot and the contestation of their throne will therefore be avoided diplomatically, so to speak.

However, if the Pharaoh doubts the claim, they must verify that the challenger isn´t in possession of the concerned card. The challenger now must turn over their card in order to show everyone that their claim was true or a bluff. They are only allowed to turn over one card. If the challenger is right, the Pharaoh is punished with two shots for distrusting their subject. If, in contrast, it was a bluff, or if the challenger can´t remember where the card is placed, they are then punished with two shots. The challenger turns their card over again.

A challenger can also make the claim that there is more than one card in their line of cards which is identical to the card in the pyramid. In this case, the number of shots is multiplied both for the Pharaoh, if they are wrong, and for the challenger, if the Pharaoh sees through their deceit.

If, for example, the challenger claims to have three jacks and the Pharaoh is right in their assumption that this is a lie, the challenger has to drink three shots. If the challenger´s claim turns out to be right, the Pharaoh has to drink six shots!

The game continues and the Pharaoh is repeatedly challenged by the other players. When all cards in the pyramid have been turned over, the reign of the Pharaoh ends and a new dynasty begins. The player left of the dying Pharaoh takes over the throne and a new game begins, the cards are reshuffled and dealt and the pyramid must now be defended by the new ruler.

## Alternatives:

An intensification of the game is possible by adding the row number of the pyramid to the number of punishment shots. For example, add one shot for each card flipped over in the bottom row (four). Add two shots, if the card is in row three, add three shots for row two and for the top card, add four shots.

In a worst case scenario the Pharaoh/challenger can be punished by 14 shots. This happens, if the following, very unlikely scenario occurs:

- The challenger claims to have three identical cards → three shots
- The top card of the pyramid is turned over → three shots + four shots for the top row = seven
- The claim is challenged by the Pharaoh (but it is true): seven shots multiplied
  by two (because of distrust) = fourteen shots
- If the Pharaoh believes the challenger however, they must drink seven shots (three identical cards + four (top row))

Note: Particularly if you choose to play the alternative version, the tension grows exponentially towards the end of the game. It can potentially become very difficult for some players. Think about lightening the game up by building a smaller pyramid with three instead of four rows, for example, or fill the shots with wine or beer instead of hard alcohol.

## Result:

Beware the Pharaoh´s curse!

# "Any questions?"

**Number of players:** 3 – 6

**Resources:** None

**Booze-factor:** Y Y

## Preparation:

All the players are sitting together in a circle. The player who usually asks the most stupid questions (that is the bimbo of the group) begins.

## Rules:

It is each player's task to ask a question to their neighbour on the left. This player is not to answer the question but instead to ask their neighbour on the left another question. This continues until one player makes a mistake.

Possible mistakes are:

**Mistake 1**  A player answers a question accidentally.

**Mistake 2**  A player repeats a question which has already been asked.

**Mistake 3**  A player takes more than three seconds to formulate question.

**Mistake 4**  A player takes too long to spit out a question. Too man "ums" and "awws" are not acceptable.

Every player who makes a mistake has to drink a shot. Their left neighbour continues the game.

## Varianten:

### (1) "No yes or no questions"

The players are not allowed to ask questions that are answered with a "yes" or "no". Whoever breaks this rule has to drink.

### (2) "Only yes or no questions"

This is the opposite of the first alternative. Only "yes or no questions" can be asked and if someone fails to do this they are punished with a shot.

### (3) "Change of order"

All types of questions are allowed. If one player asks a question which requires a longer response, the order changes and after answering that player asks the next question to the person on their right. Players who ask questions out of turn have to drink. The same goes for those players who forget to ask questions after an order change.

## Result:

At the beginning some guys might think that this game is too easy, but you will be surprised at how hard it gets, especially after a few rounds and a few drinks. It becomes very difficult to find the words and ask the right questions at the right moment.

# Gambled away

**Number of players:** 3 – 8

**Resources:** 5 die and a matchbox

**Booze-factor:**

## Preparation:

The player with the worst gambling problems, financial or casino-related, begins.

## Rules:

First only one dice is needed. The players throw, one after another, clockwise. It is their task to roll a higher number than the player before.

If one player fails to roll a higher number, they get a second chance. If they fail again, they have to drink two shots. But before throwing the second time, they have the opportunity to "buy" an additional dice. However, every dice costs one shot. The sum of the two die thrown now makes it easier for the player to beat the previous roll.

If one player buys a new a dice all the following players are allowed to use it without having to pay for it. Now two or more die are in play and the sum of the rolls are used.

Players cannot quit between rounds, they must roll a higher sum or pay (take a shot) for a new dice and thus a better chance at beating the previous number.

To prevent drinking too much you shouldn´t be that chintzy with buying new die from time to time.

At some point all five die are in the game. When this happens, players keep on playing until the first player has to drink and then the game is over. Then a new game starts again with only one dice. This rule is to prevent making one player drink continuously because the player before rolled the highest score and to roll any higher would be impossible. All die are in the game already and the player can`t improve their chances by buying more die.

## Alternatives:

### (1) "Birds of a feather flock together"

A softer version of this game can be played by counting tie rolls. If a player rolls a four for example, the next player can roll a four and escape punishment.

### (2) "Turn around Sixes"

If someone rolls only sixes with all die, the game rules change and now every player must roll a lower score in order to escape punishment. In this case they have to pay with one shot for every dice given away. If there is only one dice left the game starts again as soon as one player has been punished. The game begins with five die again. When the next six is rolled it turns back to the original rules of "higher roll wins".

### (3) "Bail yourself out"

There might be situations that make one player a repeated drinker, for example if the player before rolled two times six and two times five with four dices. Of course, the player whose turn it is can buy a fifth dice, nevertheless it will take him a long time to roll a sum over 22.
In this case they have the opportunity to bail themselves out by emptying four shots. After one player bails his way out like this the game starts again from the beginning.

**(4) "Good times – hard times"**

In some desperate situations it will help to have a joker.
Jokers can be gained by giving away die. For example, if a player rolls a very low sum such as a total of four with four die, the next player can choose to give away a dice. In return they will receive a "joker", that is a match, which they can use to miss a turn whenever they wish. The player must be confident that they can roll over the previous sum with one less dice. It is a risk and it is their choice to make.

*Optional: at the beginning of the game players can be given three matches each as "seed capital" to get out of a desperate situation.

## Result:

This game turns out to be detrimental and downright dangerous for some unfortunate fellows. According to my experience there are always one to two players every evening who are unlucky in throwing the die. Sometimes not even the matches can help them…

# Rock the office

| | |
|---|---|
| **Number of players:** | 3 or more |
| **Resources:** | Offices |
| **Partyfactor:** | ⭐⭐ |

## Preparation:

One colleague writes down all the player´s names in rows in a table. Later they will record the points for each player in their respective rows. Player´s should agree to a time frame for the game (hours, days or weeks?).

## Rules:

Players can collect points by completing the tasks given. It is important that at least one player acts as a witness. A player will only be rewarded points if they have a witness to prove the completion of every task.

**Actions rewarded with one point:**

Task 1:

The player must moan in a sexual manner for a duration of 5 minutes while in the toilet. For this task to be completed at least one non-participant (as well as a witness) must be in the toilet.

Task 2:

Men must leave their fly open for one hour as they go about their normal day in the office. Women must smear their lipstick above their lip-line, reaching their nose, and leave it there for one hour. If someone alerts the player to the fact that they look ridiculous the player must reply: "I like it better this way."

Task 3:

The player must run at full throttle once around all of the tables in the office during office hours.

Task 4:

The player must interrupt a conversation with a colleague by plugging their ears and walking away.

Task 5:

The player must walk to the coffee machine or water cooler backwards. This task must be carried out all day.

Task 6:

The player must choose one colleague that they do not know. They must call this colleague and say: "I kindly ask you to not disturb me as I'm in a meeting."

Task 7:

The player must, upon entering an elevator, take a deep, audible breath and hold it until someone exits at a floor. When someone enters or leaves the player must take a deep breath and hold it again.

Task 8:

The player must ignore the first three colleagues that greet them in the morning without saying a word.

**Actions rewarded with five points:**

Task 1:

The player must place themselves at the top of the stairs with one leg lifted in the air. They must then warn a minimum of three colleagues coming up the stairs "Be careful! You might trip!"

Task 2:

The player must use the loudspeaker system to call themselves like this: "Player's first and last name, please come to the office lobby immediately". The player may not modify their voice.

Task 3:

The player must give some instructions to an intern or new employee. The instructions should be random and incomprehensible. Then they must ask in a controlled an authoritative manner, "Did you get all of that? Because I hate to repeat myself."

Task 4:

The player must call all men "Precious" and all women "Trooper" for the whole day.

Task 5:

They player must wait until someone is giving out numbers in a meeting or over the phone. They must then shout out "69! 69! 69!" at least a half dozen times so that the whole office can hear them.

**Actions rewarded with ten points:**

Task 1:

After a good meeting or successful deal the player must, in 1970s bravado style, mime a pistol and point it at the boss while saying "You're one cool cat". Firing, blowing on the "pistol" and then returning it to its' "holster" will add the right amount of cheesiness to this task.

Task 2:

At lunch in the cafeteria the player must line up all chairs that are not being used and imitate complete with engine sounds and cheering, a Formula One race around the chairs, in which their car wins.

Task 3:

During a presentation the player must console themselves a few times by patting themselves on the back and murmuring "You're a good boy/girl. You already know all of this." If someone asks them to repeat what they've said they must talk in third person and say in an audible voice "The player's name is a good boy/girl. They already know all of this."

Task 4:

In an important telephone conference, the player must switch to street slang or cockney English and continue to talk in this manner for the rest of the conference. A few rhyming slang phrases or American gangser terms will do.

Task 5:

If some baked goods or donuts are offered in a meeting, the player must pile their plate up with all of one type (ie. jelly donuts or chocolate chip cookies) and then crumble each portion into small pieces before eating it by hand.

Task 6:

During a meeting the player must end every sentence with "fo shizzle ma nizzle". This must be repeated at least five times. Example: "Johnson, I want those numbers finished by the end of the week or you'll be fired, fo shizzle ma nizzle."

Task 7:

During a meeting the player must move slowly with their chair to make one full round of the room.

Task 8:

The player must have the following conversation with 11 different non-participants:

Player: "Hey dude, did you hear that?"

Non-participant: "What?"

Player: "Forget it, it wasn't that important!"

Task 9:

The player must weasel into a workoholics' office afterhours and switch the light on and off 11 times while they work.

Task 10:

The player must limp out of the toilet with a toilet paper train of at least one meter trailing from their pants. They should react very surprised if someone asks him about it.

Task 11:

The player has to move his feet up and down quickly during a meeting pronounce loudly that he has to leave the meeting to poop.

Task 12:

The player has to invite everyone after a meeting to put their hands together and loudly say "ommm…"

Task 13:

The player must march into the office in a military uniform and they must respond to questions stating: "Top secret. I am not allowed to talk about it."

## Alternatives:

This game can also be played in which points are not collected but the most daring participant is chosen through a vote at the end. Notes can be taken in order to remember who did what and when, and how hilarious it was.

If someone doesn´t have the heart to fulfill one of their tasks, they have to treat the others to a beer.

## Result:

Working, sex and rock´n´roll…

# Blowjob

**Number of players:**    3 – 6

**Equipment:**    Deck of cards and one glass

**Booze-factor:**    Y Y Y

## Preparation:

The glass is placed in the middle of the table and the cards are put onto the top of the glass. The player who can hold their breath the longest should become a diver. Their left neighbour starts the game.

## Rules:

The players try clockwise, one after another, to blow at least one card from the pack of cards.

If a player runs out of breath, that is to say if they are not able to blow at least one card from the pack, they must take a shot immediately. The same fate awaits the player who blows the last card from the pack of cards. They must take a shot!

There always has to be one card left on the pack before it's the next player's turn. This rule means that a player can make the next player lose (and thus drink) if they succeed in leaving only one card on the glass after their turn.

The rules in a short overview:

**Rule 1**    At least one card is to be blown from the pack of cards, or the player drinks!

**Rule 2**    At least one card has to stay on the glass, or the player drinks!

If one player breaches the rules, they are punished and the game starts again.

## Alternatives:

### (1) "Whole pack of cards"

If one player blows down the whole pack of cards at a single blow, they have to drink two shots.

### (2) "Race"

If it is one player's turn, they can blow together with the player across from them. If one of the players breaches the rules, they have to drink. If there is an uneven number of players, the player whose turn it is, can choose someone at the table to blow together with them.

### (3) "Browny"

The player whose turn it is has to put a paper bag on their head. The paper bag has a hole cut at the mouth, through which the players can blow. Consequently, the player can't see anything during their turn and has to trust their feeling not to breach the rules.

## Result:

Of course this game is a well-known classic but the proposed alternatives give it a special flavour. Unbelievable but true: there are people whose lung volume doesn't suffice for one single card after a few shots. Release them from their suffering early enough!

# Pimp my Maßkrug

**Number of players:**   3 – 8

**Equipment:**   One-litre Maßkrug, 5 shot glasses and 1 dice

**Booze-factor:**   Y Y Y

## Preparation:

For this game you need one dice, five shot glasses and one big beer steir (a traditional Maßkrug would be best). The shot glasses are placed in a row and filled up with different kinds of hard liquor. The Maß stays empty for now.

The following is a suggestion for a possible alcohol order of the shot glasses:

| Glas 1 | Glas 2 | Glas 3 | Glas 4 | Glas 5 | Maßkrug |
|--------|--------|--------|--------|--------|---------|
| ▼ | ▼ | ▼ | ▼ | ▼ | |
| Tequila | Gin | Fruit Liquor | Vodka | Jäger-meister | Empty |

## Rules:

The player who is best at simulating a drunken binge begins.
They roll the dice. The numbered rolls have the following meaning:

| | |
|---|---|
| 1 | Glass 1 (Tequila) has to be dumped into the Maß. |
| 2 | Glass 2 (Gin) has to be dumped into the Maß. |
| 3 | Glass 3 (Fruit liquor) has to be dumped into the Maß. |
| 4 | Glass 4 (Vodka) has to be dumped into the Maß. |
| 5 | Glass 5 (Jägermeister) has to be dumped into the Maß. |
| 6 | The player has to empty the Maß. |

After a glass has been dumped into the Maß, it stays empty, until its´
corresponding number is rolled again. The glass is then filled, but not
poured into the Maß until the number is rolled a third time.

If one player throws a six and the Maß is empty they are lucky and spared
from drinking.

After one player throws the dice and fulfills their actions, their left neighbor
is next.

## Alternatives:

### (1) "Continuous pimping"

As soon as one shot is dumped into the Maß the glass is refilled
immediately without waiting until its´ corresponding number is rolled
again. In this alternative the Maß is usually well-stocked before the
destructive six is rolled.

### (2) "Softpimp"

If there are decently rational people in the round, some of the glasses can
be filled with mixtures such as:

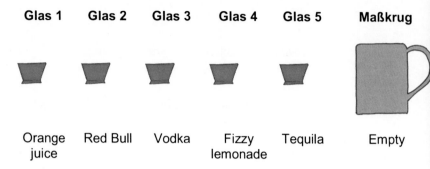

| Glas 1 | Glas 2 | Glas 3 | Glas 4 | Glas 5 | Maßkrug |
|--------|--------|--------|--------|--------|---------|
| Orange juice | Red Bull | Vodka | Fizzy lemonade | Tequila | Empty |

### (3) "Double Six"

If one player rolls a six after the player before them already rolled a six they are allowed to dump all the glasses into the Maß and choose someone to drink it. They are spared.

## Result:

Normally this game ends up in disorder and chaos.

Advice:

(1) Do not overdo it!
(2) Keep your environment clean!
(3) Pay attention to get out of this game safe!

# Father Abraham

| | |
|---|---|
| **Number of players:** | 4 – 20 |
| **Equipment:** | Big table with two benches or a lot of chairs |
| **Party-factor:** | ⭐ ⭐ ⭐ |

## Preparation:

One participant is the moderator for this game. They should already be familiar with the rules of the game in order to give the other participants a short introduction.

## Rules:

It´s the moderator´s task to sing a verse of a song with the others. The verse is the following:

"Father Abraham has seven sons, seven sons has Father Abraham. They didn´t eat anything or drink anything and they didn´t have any sorrows."

The moderator can choose any melody for the verse. They should repeat the song a few times so everyone is comfortable with it. The moderator should then shout out orders to the other participants as they sing the verse. The others must carry out the orders as they are called out. The moderator should also demonstrate the actions so they are clear.

**Here is an overview of the different orders:**

**1. Round "Left hand—right hand"**

Everyone raises their left hand and then their right.

## 2. Round "Left leg—right leg"

Everyone lifts their left leg and then their right.

## 3. Round "Slap the inside of your calves, left hand to right leg and right to left"

This action is to be repeated in round seven.

## 4. Round "Lift your legs and kick your feet"

## 5. Round "Up and down"

Everyone stands up and sits down continuously as they sing.

## 6. Round "Ass up"

Everyone bounces their ass up and down on the bench continuously into the next round.

## 7. Round "Tongue out"

Everyone makes the movement of rounds three and six, sticking out their tongues between the words of the verse.

# Alternatives:

The moderator and other participants can think up some other movements to combine in order to up the party factor in the next rounds.

# Result:

In testing all participants ended up falling off their chairs in laughter after round seven.

# Fire breather

**Number of players:**   3 – 8

**Resources:**   One dice for each player, several packs of superhot chili-flavoured or barbeque chips and Tabasco sauce

**Booze-factor:**   Y Y Y

## Preparation:

There are no non-alcoholic drinks allowed at the table for this game. Teams of any size are formed in any order among the players. Ideally the players of one team sit together.

## Rules:

Each player throws their dice. If the number rolled is a 4, 5 or 6, the player goes on to the next round and their team is still in the running. If the player rolls a 1, 2 or 3, they are out and they have to eat one of the very hot chips as punishment. A team only stays in the game if at least one team member throws successfully. The triumphant player(s) of that team stays in the game and is allowed to roll the dice again.

When the last player of one team fails to roll a 4 or higher the entire team is disqualified and the remaining teams keep on playing.

The last team remaining in the game is the winning team. They now roll to decide on the punishment for the losing team(s). Every player of the winning team who has lasted until the final round throws their dice. The numbers on the die are summed up and represent the number of hot chips each player of the losing team has to eat. The winning team is saved from eating any of the chips and celebrates its´ victory.

After a spicy feast for the losing team, the game starts again from the beginning and each team is allowed to roll the die again.

## Alternatives:

### (1) "3-2-1"

Each player has three chances in the first round to roll a 4, 5 or 6. If they manage to move on, they have two more chances in round two and one chance to succeed in the last round(s). This alternative makes the game easier.

### (2) "Wild Fire"

If in a round more than one player fails to roll a 4, 5 or 6, the failed player must as many chips as there are failed players on their team.
Example: If three players of the same team fail in one round, then each of the three failed players has to eat three chips.

### (3) "Red-hot"

In this alternative the feared Tabasco bottle comes into the game. The losing teams are additionally punished by getting a shot of Tabasco on each of their chips.

## Result:

After reading the rules, one might ask themself, why is there a booze-factor in this game? The reason is that after a few rounds of chip-eating, everyone will need to quench their thirst by drinking! Unfortunately booze is not the best drink for the job.

Note: By ensuring that only alcoholic drinks are present during this game you will guarantee a good time!

# Sardine

**Number of players:** 4 – 8

**Equipment:** A bottle of wine

**Booze-factor:** ▼ ▼

## Preparation:

The player who provided the bottle of wine takes it and hides themselves somewhere in the surroundings (if you play in a big house, cupboards, extra rooms, under the bed, the roof are good places to hide, if you have open space then you have endless choices).

## Rules:

After waiting for five minutes the remaining players grab a glass and start searching for the wine bandit. If one player locates the bandit, they can help themselves to a glass of wine with the bandit.

This continues for as long as it takes all the players to find the bandit or until the bottle is empty and a new round begins.

## Alternatives:

### "Oiled sardine"

In addition to the wine bottle the bandit takes a box of sardines and a bottle of suntan oil.
The first player who locates the bandit is rewarded with a glass of wine.

The second one has to eat a sardine and the third player´s face is smeared with suntan lotion. The following player gets a glass of wine again and the pattern repeats itself. The game lasts longer this way and is more ridiculous.

As before, the game is finished when all players have located the bandit´s hiding place or when there is no wine left.

## Result:

"Im Dunkeln ist gut Munkeln"

# Dirty Talk

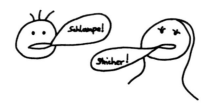

| | |
|---|---|
| **Number of players:** | 4 – 6 |
| **Equipment:** | Presence of some "non-participants" |
| **Booze-factor:** | ▼ ▼ |

## Preparation:

The players search for a place in a crowd. This could ideally be a Bavarian "beergarden" or some other festival in which booze is the focus.

The nastiest, dirtiest player begins.

## Rules:

The first player has to shout a dirty word or something nasty into the crowd, like for example "bitch". They have to be clever enough so that no one in the crowd realizes who shouted the dirty word and they are not held accountable for it. If they fail, and are noticed, they have to drink a shot.

They also have to drink if they call out the word too quietly. It has to be audible to the others around. The whole group of players decides whether the player has broken this rule or not. After every exclamation the task moves clockwise to the next player.

# Alternatives:

## "Town Crier"

Now the goal is to make at least one non-participant react in an obvious way to your dirty exclamation. Whoever doesn't manage this, has to drink, of course!

# Result:

It is recommended to change scenery from time to time because after a few rounds there won't be any more reactions from the crowd and it becomes too easy to fulfil the task.

# Chinese Whispers

| | |
|---|---|
| **Number of players:** | 4 – 8 |
| **Equipment:** | Pen and paper |
| **Booze-factor:** | ⭐⭐ |

## Preparation:

For this game you need a pen and a piece of paper.

The player who can draw the best has to choose a common phrase/expression.

## Rules:

The expression chosen is whispered into the ear of the player's left neighbour, similar to the popular game of "Chinese Whispers" or "Broken Telephone". The phrase may only be whispered once.

The neighbour now has to draw this phrase onto a piece of paper. No other player is allowed to watch them draw. When finished, the drawer hands over their drawing to their neighbour on the left. This player now tries to derive the phrase/expression in question from the drawing and then whispers what they think the phrase is into their neighbour's ear.

As the game goes around the table the phrase is passed on by drawers and whisperers in turn until the final player in the circle has been reached. It's now this player's turn to say the phrase out loud. To finish, the original expression is revealed.

## Alternatives:

### "Message in a bottle"

This game can easily be turned into a great drinking game. For this, each player has to note down the expression they understood or derived from the drawing.

After revealing both terms at the end of the game, all players have to show the expressions they noted down. Each wrong phrase equals one drink.

## Result:

Heavy drinkers often are great artists…

# Aunt Mary

**Number of players:**   3 – 5

**Equipment:**   1 pack of toothpicks

**Booze-factor:**

## Preparation:

Each player receives a toothpick and breaks off the pointy ends. Players insert the toothpicks horizontally into their mouths so that the toothpicks reach from cheek to cheek.

## Rules:

The player with the worst breath starts.

They turn to the player to their left and say: ‚Have you heard? Aunt Mary is sick." Their Neighbour responds with "What's wrong with her?" The first player replies with a disease of their choice, for example the chickenpox. This ends the dialogue.

The player to the left now becomes the new player and repeats the dialogue with the person to their left. Upon being asked "What's wrong with her?" they also choose a disease. However, they first need to repeat all previously mentioned diseases.

A player is punished by having to drink a shot if they break one of the following rules:

1) The player makes a mistake in the sequence of diseases and lists them in the wrong order

2) The players can't remember all diseases or forgets to mention one or more

3) The player cannot come up with a new disease for Aunt Mary to suffer (Author's Note: I have never witnessed this happen – there are just too many possibilities ☺)

After every dialogue, the dialogue moves clockwise onto the next person and to each disease, another one is added.

The toothpicks are kept in the mouths throughout the whole game. The only time they should be removed is to drink in order to avoid a possibility of choking.

## Alternatives:

**"What's up?"**

All players insert the toothpicks upright – vertically – from tongue to roof of mouth.

This makes speaking even harder – diseases are so hard to understand that they become impossible to repeat. This naturally results in more drinking.

## Result:

"Here's to Aunt Mary's health!"

# Panamericana

**Number of players:**   4 – 8

**Resources:**   Writing pad, pencils and two die

**Booze-factor:**

## Preparation:

Each player gets one writing pad on which they draws three small boxes in a row.

The player who lives in the house with the highest street number begins.

## Rules:

The object of the game is to obtain the highest street number possible. They throw the dice. The rolled number is recorded in one of the three boxes. Each player should be strategic about where they put their numbers, higher numbers should be placed first in the row.

Each player rolls the dice once and passes it to their left neighbour. After everyone has rolled three times the 'street numbers' (that is, the lowest number in the row of boxes) are evaluated.

The player with the lowest street number loses and gets punished with a shot.

## Alternatives:

### (1) "At the end of the street"

The game reverses, the player with the highest street number has to drink.

### (2) "Action-dice"

A second dice enters the game. A player rolls the first dice and writes their number in the box. Then they roll the second, so called "action-dice"

The numbers rolled for the action-dice have the following meaning:

### Number 1:

The action-dice is blocked for the following player, they can only use the first dice.

### Number 2:

The player is allowed to throw the action-dice a second time.

### Number 3:

The player has to exchange their writing pad with their left neighbour.

### Number 4:

The player has to exchange their writing pad with their right neighbour.

### Number 5:

The player is allowed to cross out a box of any player. They, therefore have the possibility to lower the street number of the leading player significantly.

### Number 6:

The player is allowed to draw one new box on the left or the right side of their existing boxes.

## Result:

"Allee, Allee, Allee, Allee – eine Straße mit viele Bäumen, ja das ist eine Allee!"

# Beerathlon

| | |
|---|---|
| **Number of players:** | 10 or more |
| **Equipment:** | 1 box of beer per team |
| **Booze-factor:** |  |

## Preparation:

Players are divided into teams of two. It's up to you whether you want to draw teams or whether players can make up the teams themselves.

For the beerathlon a route of about 5 to 10 kilometers should be chosen.

## Rules:

Each team takes one box of beer.

The task is to race the designated route with that box of beer. The beer bottles can be emptied during the race, but only if they are drunk. All teams can decide on carrying the box with full, half-full or even empty bottles of beer - as long as they make it to the finish line.

It's possible to carry the box either in turns or together at all times. Again this is a decision to be made by each team. Often these "strategies" end up being tossed out the window anyway… The winner of the beerathlon is the team that crosses the finish line first.

Important note: The beer box must cross the finish line with all bottles. However, it doesn't matter whether they are full, half-full or empty. Of course, no form of vehicles or wheeled objects are allowed.

## Alternatives:

### "Empty bottle"

This alternative, named after famous Italian soccer trainer Giovanni Trappatoni, requires all teams to empty their box before crossing the finishing line.

In order to makes this a valid alternative for all, not just the heavy drinkers among you, teams can be stocked up to four members or teams of two can use a keg instead of an entire box.

## Result:

This game is especially popular with soccer teams. In case there are female players willing to try, we recommend participating men to behave like gentlemen and to let them use a box of either light beer or smaller bottles.

Extensive beerathlon history has shown that teams tend to "fall apart" quickly throughout the game. For the sake of amusement, it may therefore be useful to put up guards at certain points of the route to note down the time each team took for the different sections and take photos for the beerathlon archives.

# Witch Hunt

**Number of Players:**     4 – 12

**Equipment:**     2 die, 1 bandana and 1 apron

**Booze-factor:**

## Preparation:

The player with biggest nose begins.

## Rules:

The beginner rolls one of the dice. At the same time, the player sitting directly across from them rolls the other dice.

If one of the players rolls a 6, they pass the dice on to the person on their left. If not, they keep going until the player rolls a 6. The dice are continually rolled for sixes and passed to the left until one person has both dice – the die have caught up with each other.

The witch has been found!

The player who receives both dice has to wear the bandana and the apron. Of course, the witch also has to have a drink.

The next round begins with the witch rolling one dice and the player sitting opposite rolling the other. The bandana and apron can only be taken off once the new witch is found.

## Alternatives:

### (1) "Witches' Night"

The players no longer roll the dice simultaneously – rather, players try to roll a 6 as fast as possible, in order to not be the next witch.

### (2) "Black Cat"

In addition to the dice being passed to the left once a 6 is rolled, the dice is passed to the right when a 1 is rolled.

### (3) "Curse"

If two players sitting next to each other both roll a 6, the player who rolled it last must drink.

## Result:

Mount your brooms!

# Bier Roulette

**Number of Players:** 2 or more players

**Equipment:** Several identical beer cans

**Booze-factor:** ▼ ▼ ▼

## Preparation:

Each player has a beer can. The player with the most gambling debts begins.

All players have to stand in a line.

## Rules:

Every participant picks up a beer can, but only the first player is allowed to shake their can. Afterwards the cans are placed on a table and mixed. After mixing up the cans no one should know which can is the one that was shaken.

Now one after the other, each player picks up a can, holds it to their mouth and opens it.

One of the players will be surprised with a beer shower!

## Alternatives:

**(1) "50:50"**

Every second player is allowed to shake their beer can.

**(2) "Foreign hand"**

The rules of the previous alternative are followed, but for this variation the left neighbour opens the can into the mouth of each player.

## Result:

Beer Roulette belongs to the category of classical drinking games which are often played on hot days during music festivals.

# Beer Coaster Ninja

**Number of players::**   3 – 8

**Equipment:**   Beer glasses and beer coasters

**Booze-factor:**

## Preparation:

Every player gets one beer glass and two coasters. They place the beer glass in front of them and put one of the coasters on top. The other coaster serves as their missile.

## Rules:

The ninja who has the strongest calves*, is first to try their luck.

*Bavarian chicks find strong calves very attractive, hence the lederhosen which shows them off nicely. Don´t ask.

Players stand an agreed distance back from the table. The studly first player takes the second coaster and tries to knock another player´s coaster off their glass. If they are successful, the player whose coaster has been dislodged has to take a shot immediately and then put the coaster back on their glass again.

In case of a miss, it´s the next player´s turn.

## Alternatives:

### (1) "Dojo"

If one player's beer coaster is knocked off, the punishment is not only to take a shot but also they must put another beer coaster on the top of their glass. This results in "stacking" of beer coasters. In the next round if both (or all) coasters are knocked off the player is punished with an equal number of shots.

Sometimes, beer coasters pile up on top of one player's glass. With every additional beer coaster the target becomes bigger and easier for the other ninjas to attack.

### (2) "Kamikaze"

Each player is given more beer coaster missiles (for example five). All players are allowed to shoot at the same time in order to knock off any player's coaster. If someone succeeds, the game is stopped for a quick shot and the affected player has to drink. If one player runs out of coasters they can just pick up one of the coasters lying around and keep on firing.

## Result:

"Hajime!"

# Corporate Poker

**Number of players:**      6

**Equipment:**      1 deck of cards, 1 piece of paper, 1 pen

**Party-factor:**      ★ ★ ★

## Preparation:

The paper is cut into six equal pieces and the following is written on them

Paper 1: Boss
Paper 2: Manager
Paper 3: Department Head
Paper 4: Secretary
Paper 5: Intern
Paper 6: Dishwasher

This game can be played with less players – positions just need to be removed accordingly.

Once the papers are ready, they are folded and put into a container and mixed thoroughly. Each player picks a piece of paper – that will be the position each player starts with.

The boss picks a place to sit at the beginning of each round. All other players sit around him according to their positions: the manager to the left of the boss, the department head to the left of the manager, the secretary to the left of the department head, etc.

The deck is shuffled and 13 cards are dealt out to each player. The playe with the lowest rank (the dishwasher) receives 14. The remaining cards are put to the side.

## Rules:

The goal is to get rid of the dealt cards as quickly as possible.

The high-ranked players enjoy certain privileges: the boss gets the dishwasher's two highest cards. In exchange, the dishwasher receives the boss's two lowest cards. The manager gets the intern's highest card in exchange for their lowest card. The department head and secretary keep their hands.

Cards are ranked as follows, highest to lowest:

Joker, Ace, King, Queen, Jack, 10, 9, 8, 7, 6, 5, 4, 3, 2

The highest ranking players also have other privileges – the boss and manager never shuffle or deal cards. This becomes the dishwasher's role. Also, the dishwasher is responsible for filling up drinks and bringing food to the table, should anything run out.

The game begins after all cards are exchanged. The boss goes first – they can either play one card or multiple cards. However, multiple cards can only be played if they have the same value (e.g. three Jacks). Tactically, playing the lowest cards first makes most sense as it saves the higher ones for later play-offs.

After the boss plays, the closest in rank follows.

Players can choose if they want to play a card or pass. Should players choose to play a card, it must have a higher value than the one played previously. For example, if the department head plays a 10, the intern must play a Jack or higher.

Furthermore, the multiples must coincide – three Queens must be followed by three Kings or higher.

In the event that all players pass on a card, the player who laid down the last cards gets to turn over the accumulated pile and start over. The advantage of this is that they can lay the first card regardless of their rank and lose their lowest cards that way.

Each player should strive to play the highest card in the round in order to win such an opportunity. However, tactically speaking, this does not mean that the highest cards should be played first. This would make play-offs later in the game impossible to win. Ideally, the game is carefully observed in order to predict what high cards are still in the game.

The Joker is the highest card. It cannot be beaten – if the Joker is played, the pile is automatically turned over and the player who put down the Joker may begin again. Furthermore, the Joker is also a wild card – it can stand in for any card while playing multiples. For example, if a player puts down 4 nines and a Joker, the next player can only beat this with 5 tens.

In order to illustrate the rules, below are two sample rounds that could be played:

### Round 1:

Boss plays 2 fours
-> Manager plays 2 fives
-> Department head plays 2 nines
-> Secretary plays 2 tens
-> Intern passes (and doesn't put down any cards)
-> Dishwasher passes
-> Boss plays 2 Jacks
-> Manager plays 1 King and 1 Joker (=2 Kings)
-> Department head passes
-> Intern passes
-> Dishwasher passes
-> Boss passes

The Manager wins this play-off. He gets to turn the pile over and play the next cards.

### Round 2:

-> Manager plays 1 Jack
-> Department head plays 1 Queen

-> Secretary plays 1 King
-> Intern passes
-> Dishwasher passes
-> Boss plays a Joker

The boss wins with the Joker and may turn over the existing pile to start a new one.

The first person to lay down all their cards wins the round and automatically assumes the position of the boss for the next round. All remaining players continue playing out for the subsequent positions until only one player remains. This player becomes the dishwasher.

It is possible to change rank from round to round.

A small tactical hint: players should try to assume the position above them by attempting to beat that person in the play-offs. Should the higher rank remain unaffected or keep beating the rounds, it may be best to change tactics and defend their own position.

## Alternatives:

### (1) "Report to the office!"

As soon as the first player finishes their hand, the game is over. That player becomes the boss for the next round.

The remaining cards in each player's hand determine the following ranks. The player with the lowest remaining cards assumes the position of the Manager; the player with the second lowest remaining cards becomes the department head, etc.

If two players have the same amount of cards left over, the player with the lower rank from the last round assumes the higher position for the next round. For example, if the intern and the dishwasher each have six cards left, the dishwasher becomes the intern and the intern the dishwasher for the next round.

## Result:

"Time to climb the corporate ladder!"

# Titanic

**Number of players:** 3 – 6

**Equipment:** Maß (beer stein), 0.2l glass (whiskey glass or tumbler), bottles of beer

**Booze-/Party-factor:** 

## Preparation:

The Maß is filled up with beer and the glass is then put into the Maß – much like a boat sailing in a beer ocean. Each player needs a bottle of beer.

## Rules:

Whoever has had an affair with either Kate Winslet and/or Leonardo Di Caprio or their doppelgangers should start the game.

The first player pours a little bit out of their beer bottle into the empty glass swimming in the Maß. Clockwise, all subsequent players will do the same until the glass sinks. The player who sunk the ship must now retrieve the glass from the bottom of the Maß, fill it up with beer and drink it.

A new round begins and the now empty glass is put into the Maß again – much like a boat in a beer ocean. ☺

## Alternatives:

### (1) "Full Freight"

A dice as well as six shot glasses are needed. All shot glasses are filled up with beer.

The players throw the dice in turn. The numbers they roll indicate the number of shot glasses each player has to pour into the glass swimming in the Maß. It is therefore crucial to roll low numbers in order to avoid pouring too many shot glasses into the "boat in the ocean" which will make it much more likely to sink to the bottom of beer sea. ☺

### (2) "Ship ahoy!"

The 0.2l glass is put into an empty Maß. Also, a packet of sherbet is emptied into the glass. One after another, all players now pour a little bit of sparkling (mineral) water into the glass. The player who causes the glass to foam over has to drink what is called a porno-vodka (a shot of vodka together with a packet of sherbet, preferably the German brand "Ahoj").

## Result:

It's just a matter of time until the captain leaves the sinking ship!

# Agro stork

**Number of players:**  3 – 6

**Resources:**  1 dice and condoms

**Booze-factor:**

## Preparation:

The dice is stuffed into a condom (or balloon) and then it is blown up and tied. The more air you put in it the faster the game goes.

The player who can claim the most Bavarian heritage begins.

## Rules:

The player rolls the dice by tossing the condom/balloon on a table. It is important to ensure that the dice moves. If that doesn´t happen the first rule is broken and the player has to empty a shot.

The rolled numbers have the following meaning:

**Number 1:**

The player has to shake the condom violently for 10 seconds and if doesn´t burst they must then pass it to the player across from them.

**Number 2:**

The player must roll the dice a second time by tossing the

condom/balloon.

## Number 3:

The players continue the game, now rolling the dice clockwise (if that is not already the case).

## Number 4:

The players continue the game, now rolling the dice counter-clockwise (if that is not already the case).

## Number 5:

The condom is passed from player to player once around the table. If it bursts in the hands of a player that player must drink. If it bursts between two players the others must decide which of them has to drink.

## Number 6:

The player has to throw the condom/balloon into the air and shout *"Prost! damit die Gurgel nicht verrostet!"* and catch it again. If it bursts they have to fulfill their prophecy.

General rule: If the condom/balloon bursts, the responsible player is punished and a new round starts.

# Alternatives:

### (1) "Prickly friend"

A little cactus is put in the middle of the table. If a player rolls a 6 they must drop the condom/balloon onto the cactus from a short height.
All the players (including the one whose turn it is) can influence the flight path of the condom/balloon by blowing on it heavily.

If the player is lucky and the condom/balloon misses the cactus they are saved. If the condom/balloon bursts however, they have to drink.

**(2) "Fatass"**

If a player rolls a 5 he can choose someone to sit on the condom/balloon. After the condom/balloon inevitably bursts, that player drinks and a new round begins.

## Result:

Please throw away the condoms after the game because if you don't the agro stork might visit you later!

# Bavarian – English

| | |
|---|---|
| **Maßkrug** | Beer stein (Bavarians are used to drinking beer from a 1 liter beer stein when they go to the October Festival or to the beergarden). |
| **Bierdeckel** | Beer coaster (is often abused for spontaneous games). |
| **Dirndl** | A traditional Bavarian dress that enhances the girls' figure and cleavage. |
| **Lederhose** | Traditional Bavarian short trousers made out of leather that Bavarian men wear as often as they can (e.g. Champions League final, beer festivals). |
| **Schuhblattler** | Men in Lederhosen who perform a traditional Bavarian dance in which they slap their thighs and feet. See youtube! |
| **König Ludwig II** | The Bavarian king who lived from 1845 to 1886. He built a couple of fantasy castles (among other things Neuschwanstein castle). He was a romantic and quite possible Wagner´s lover. |
| **Wolpertinger** | This is a fictional animal said to inhabit the alpine forests of Bavaria in Germany. It has a body comprised from various animals (http://en.wikipedia.org/wiki/Wolpertinger). |
| **Schadenfreude** | More German than Bavarian and means "malicious smirk" but is also "schadenfreude" in English ☺ |
| **„Prost, damit die Gurgel nicht verost!"** | Literal translation: "Cheers! Let's avoid that our throats get rusty!" |
| **„Petri heil!"** | More German than Bavarian and means "good luck while fishing!" |
| **„Allee, Allee, Allee, Allee – eine Straße mit viele Bäumen, ja das ist eine Allee!"** | Literal translation: "Alley, alley, alley, alley – a street with lots of trees that's an alley!"<br><br>This verse is part of a popular song that people sing in beer tents at Octoberfest as well as during any soccer event. |

| | |
|---|---|
| **„Im Dunkeln ist gut Munkeln"** | The dark makes for more fun. |
| **„Lass sie bluten"** | Literal translation: "Let them bleed!" |

# International Toasts

| | |
|---|---|
| **Albania:** | Gëzuar! |
| **Australia:** | Cheers mate! |
| **Brazil:** | Saúde! |
| **Bolivia:** | Arriba - abajo – al centro – al dentro! |
| **Bulgaria:** | Nasdrave! |
| **China:** | Gan bei! |
| **Canada:** | Cheers! |
| **Denmark:** | Skål |
| **Germany:** | Prost! |
| **England:** | Cheers! |
| **Esperanto:** | Je via sano! |
| **Estonia:** | Terviseks! |
| **Finland:** | Kippis! |
| **France:** | (A votre) Santé! |
| **Georgia:** | Gaumardjos |
| **Greece:** | Jámas! |
| **Ireand:** | Sláinte! |
| **Iceland:** | Skål |
| **Israel:** | L´cháim! |
| **Italy:** | Salute! |
| **Japan:** | Kampai! |

| | |
|---|---|
| **Korea:** | Geonbae! |
| **Cuba:** | Salud, amór y dinéro! |
| **Latvia:** | Priekā! |
| **Lithuania:** | Sveikatą! |
| **Luxemburg:** | Prost! |
| **Malta:** | Evviva! |
| **Netherlands:** | Proost! |
| **Norway:** | Skål! |
| **Austria:** | Proscht! |
| **Poland:** | (Na) zdrowie! |
| **Portugal:** | Saúde! |
| **Romania:** | Noroc! |
| **Russia:** | Nazdarovje! |
| **Scotland:** | Slainte mhath! |
| **Sweden:** | Skål |
| **Switzerland:** | Proscht! |
| **Serbia:** | Na Zdravlje! |
| **Scandinavia:** | Skål |
| **Slovakia:** | Nazdravie! |
| **Slovenia:** | Na zdravje! |
| **Spain:** | Salud! |
| **Czech Republic:** | Na zdraví! |
| **Turkey:** | Şerefe! |

| | |
|---|---|
| **Ukraine:** | Budmo! |
| **Hungary:** | Egészségére! |
| **United States:** | Cheers! |
| **Wales:** | Lechyd da! |

# Famous Drinking Quotes:

### 1. George Jean Nathan [1882-1958]:

*"I drink to make other people interesting."*


### 2. Ernest Hemingway [1899-1961]

*"Drinking is a way of ending the day."*


### 3. Frank Sinatra [1915-98]

*"I feel sorry for people who don't drink. When they wake up in the morning, that's as good as they're going to feel all day."*


### 4. Tom Waits [1949- ]

*"I'd rather have a free bottle in front of me than a prefrontal lobotomy."* [Editor's Note: This quote has been widely attributed to Dorothy Parker.]


### 5. Anonymous

*"Reality is an illusion that occurs due to the lack of alcohol."*

## 6. Dean Martin [1917-95]

*"You're not drunk if you can lie on the floor without holding on."*

## 7. Billy Carter [1937-88]

*"Beer is not a good cocktail-party drink, especially in a home where you don't know where the bathroom is."*

## 8. W.C. Fields [1880-1946]

*"Somebody left the cork out of my lunch."*

## 9. Charles Bukowski [1920-94]

*"There was nothing really as glorious as a good beer shit - I mean after drinking twenty or twenty-five beers the night before. The odor of a beer shit like that spread all around and stayed for a good hour-and-a-half. It made you realize that you were really alive."*

## 10. Dylan Thomas [1914-53]

*"An alcoholic is someone you don't like who drinks as much as you do."*